Cross-Brand Yourself
Think Outside Your Niche

An Introductory Handbook Guide

Into the Basics of Cross-Branding

Alicia "WATERS"

CROSS-BRAND YOURSELF

For ordering, booking, permission, or questions, contact the author.
www.anwempires@gmail.com
www.amazon.com/author/alicianwaters

ISBN:13: 978-1533661159

Printed in the United States of America by Create Space

CROSS-BRAND YOURSELF

Cross-Brand Yourself

Think Outside Your Niche

As a cross industries entrepreneur, serving in roles such as cross-niche journalist/marketer and crossover industries branding strategist, I see several entrepreneurs who experience the feast or famine cycle in their businesses. Often, this happens because they limit themselves by only marketing to serve in one target market. This is why the next revolution of entrepreneurial change will begin with redefining business and marketing success through cross-branding with other main and sub-niches. This will allow entrepreneurs to showcase their personal brand, products and/or services in various ways to multiple industries.

Like several, I also experienced the seasons of what seemed like just famines without the feast. This experience felt more like receiving an occasional snack or having a good friend offer to pay for your meal every now and then.

I know that the gurus tell us that we should find our niche and stick to serving that audience. I agree, that you certainly need a primary focus for an audience; however, I don't believe that you are limited to just serving in one arena. This is why it's time to cross-brand yourself and think outside of just your traditional target market. Your brand is you and you are not just limited to a target audience.

Again, most limit themselves to being a one-brand or one-niche-wonder. Entrepreneurs have to begin to see their entire experience as the foundation that makes up their brand and not just an area of expertise. There are many facets to our capabilities and it's time to use all of it to elevate our business frameworks.

New era entrepreneurs must learn how to operate in the energy of what I call, *conscious multiplicity,* in order to re-purpose what they already do and cross-market their efforts and endeavors in different industries. This concept not only increases your impact, but also your income, and keeps you out of the feast or famine cycle.

This awareness shifted me into a more expanded perspective for establishing an empire that would not only produce a feast but a habitation for continued opulence.   I knew that this new way of doing business would allow me to showcase all of my skills and passions in various ways at different times. This process became an evolutionary journey of learning how to become an alchemist to transform lead into to gold and remix what was possible as an entrepreneur.

Over the years, I got tired of hearing so-called experts say that you can't serve in multiple arenas; however, I knew that my soul was telling me that I was called for this experience. I had to keep pressing through to creatively discover a way that I could maximize my efforts to show up as a non-linear cross industries entrepreneur.

CROSS-BRAND YOURSELF

So I began re-establishing myself as a business expression for being the empire itself, versus just building one. This involved me using all of my personal, professional and spiritual experiences as life's cross-training mastery academy so that I could position myself as a holistic lifestyle and business authority for serving in other arenas that I desired.

If you're not familiar with cross-branding, in short, cross-branding is simply displaying or showcasing one's brand or talent in multiple ways to appeal to different audiences or bringing forth another aspect of their non-dominant offerings or roles to serve in different arenas outside of their traditional niche/target market. Some of the benefits of cross-branding are it involves cross-promotions or cross-merchandising. This allows for not only a re-purposing of an entrepreneur's brand, but also their products or services to gain exposure with others outside their traditional market.

Cross-merchandising provides the ability to repackage or re-purpose your offers through cross-marketing. Again this gives people who traditionally would not be interested in the title of your product or the way that you've showcased it in another arena. There might be one aspect of your signature work or another non-dominant area of your gifting that you can look at from a higher perspective or different vantage point to see if that one element can stand on its own as part of your cross-branding efforts to serve another industry. Again, you can take one concept, product or service and creatively make it marketable for other arenas.

CROSS-BRAND YOURSELF

Some might think this process seems overwhelming, especially if you want to showcase multiple skills. However, it's all about being simplistic, aligned and organized. Serving in various venues doesn't mean that you're all over the place all the time. There is an old saying; "You can do everything and have it all, just not all at once." Serving for various industries allows you to be very flexible with your endeavors and run your entrepreneurial expressions like a University that only offers certain courses or events at certain times every year or every other year.

This type of business framework allows you to create success your way while making an impact and residual income all year round. I once the heard speaker, Adam King say; "You can create the life you want on your own terms. All you need is perspective."

Again, this new era of business and marketing evolution will be elevated through cross-industry entrepreneurs who are showing up as authentic business expressions or as cross-branded movements. My entrepreneurial expression is called The Total ME Empires, which allows me to become less institutionalized in my business dynamics. This way I get to use everything I have in my arsenal within my business frameworks.

CROSS-BRAND YOURSELF

Even if entrepreneurs are already knowledgeable about cross-branding, my goal is to create an elevated awareness for next level pioneers to be knowledgeable for learning how to thrive above the feast or famine season in their businesses by fully showing up using multiple areas of their unique talents. Utilizing their multiple passions will allow them to make a huge impact and a lucrative income from doing not only what they love, but also from being the person that they would love to be as an expression in the world.

As I mentioned previously, you are your brand, but also you are your business empire. If you're limiting your brand-ability to cross-market, you will more than likely continue to limit your opportunities for infinite prosperity. Instead, you'll remain stagnant or only evolve in your small container of a limited entrepreneurial paradigm.

CROSS-BRAND YOURSELF

A simple call to action to begin cross-branding yourself and thinking outside your niche, starts with asking yourself empowering questions.

Questions &/or Actions to Consider:

I'm curious to know what other industries are hungry for what I have to offer?

I'm wondering if there is an aspect of my work that I can re-purpose and make it marketable to another industry? If so, what would that be?

How can I think outside my niche or my resume to cross-brand/market myself?

CROSS-BRAND YOURSELF

Here are some basics to help you become effective through using the art of simplicity.

3 Simple Call to Actions to Get Started:

1. Spend some reflection time brainstorming ways to cross-market your products and services into other industries.

2. Decide what industries you desire to serve in outside your niche and then find out what the minimum requirements are to start at an entry-level for positioning yourself in that arena.

3. Spend some time researching the anthropology of your new market to discover creative ways to communicate about what you do and what you offer for them. Because they are outside of your traditional market, you must examine how you can re-purpose your title or benefits to attract them. After you've followed these steps begin to formulate a marketing plan of action.

Always think outside your niche and go beyond yourself as a BRAND!

CROSS-BRAND YOURSELF

Easy & Effective Ways to Begin Cross-Branding Yourself

1. **Write for the industries that you desire to serve and position yourself as an expert**: You can write your way into any industry as an entry point to gain credibility. Most top industry leaders respect published works. Create a new blog, e-zine and/or a mini-book to introduce yourself to your new audience. Begin to leverage your physical and/or digital writings as nonlinear business cards to your prospects or Joint Ventures.

2. **Discover what are the basic entry-level requirements**: If you don't have any formal training in certain areas, get the basic entry-level certificate or diploma that might be required. If no formal training is required, if you're not interested or don't have time for formal training then take a mini-course, teleclass or once again, get published. You can also create an audio product from a teleseminar that you've done and/or a video training series on YouTube from your areas of expertise or passions to use as an entry point.

CROSS-BRAND YOURSELF

3. **Reinterpret & Re-purpose your professional resume and life experiences**: Re-examine your resume and/or professional experiences by looking at your dominate roles within your present or former job descriptions to see if any of those areas will assist you with your cross-branding efforts.

This process will also help you to become more aware of how to elevate your expertise through building a portfolio that incorporates certain aspects from your holistic life experience to use as leverage towards your professional credibility. This will help you to discover that you've already established your expertise in several areas, just in a nonlinear or informal training process.

Again, it's time to cross-brand yourself and think outside the niche. Explore and inventory your offerings and/or consider something that you've never thought of before to create a new entrepreneurial adventure.

Use the concepts in this handbook to help you design an entry level action plan. When you're ready to up-level and design a business model for cross-branding yourself effectively, visit www.crossbrandingyounow.tumblr.com in order to get information about being mentored through a high-level mastermind.

Becoming a cross-niche or cross-industries entrepreneur is not a process that you need to try alone. The concepts in this handbook will get you started and will help you to achieve great results. However, if you're wanting to do this full time and design a lifestyle entrepreneurial model, you must get expert help to create a scalable, sustainable and structure system for success.

The best way to use this handbook to design your next steps for cross-branding is to be consistent with brainstorming and writing down every idea that comes to you without trying to edit. Write out articles, blogs and even your book projects in the action planning section. Re-read the handbook several times and only working on one or two recommendations at a time that resonate with you the most in the present.

It's best to design a 90-day action plan that is broken down into three 30 day phases to monitor your entry-level success. Rinse and repeat the process in order to create the consistent results that you want. Even with the basic entry-level concepts shared in this handbook, you can create a simple business model that can position you for better opportunities. However, as mentioned previously, if you desire to create a full-time lifestyle entrepreneurial venture through your cross-branding efforts, you will need a high-level mentor and cross industries expert to help you develop your empire.

Cross Brand Yourself

Think Outside Your Niche

Action Planning Section

Brainstorming & Action Planning

Brainstorming & Action Planning

Brainstorming & Action Planning

Brainstorming & Action Planning

Brainstorming & Action Planning

CROSS-BRAND YOURSELF

Brainstorming & Action Planning

Brainstorming & Action Planning

Brainstorming & Action Planning

Brainstorming & Action Planning

Brainstorming & Action Planning

Brainstorming & Action Planning

Brainstorming & Action Planning

Brainstorming & Action Planning

Brainstorming & Action Planning

Brainstorming & Action Planning

Brainstorming & Action Planning

Brainstorming & Action Planning

Brainstorming & Action Planning

Brainstorming & Action Planning

Brainstorming & Action Planning

Brainstorming & Action Planning

Brainstorming & Action Planning

Brainstorming & Action Planning

Brainstorming & Action Planning

Brainstorming & Action Planning

Brainstorming & Action Planning

Brainstorming & Action Planning

Brainstorming & Action Planning

Brainstorming & Action Planning

Brainstorming & Action Planning

Brainstorming & Action Planning

Brainstorming & Action Planning

Brainstorming & Action Planning

Brainstorming & Action Planning

Brainstorming & Action Planning

Brainstorming & Action Planning

Brainstorming & Action Planning

CROSS-BRAND YOURSELF

Brainstorming & Action Planning

Brainstorming & Action Planning

Brainstorming & Action Planning

Brainstorming & Action Planning

Brainstorming & Action Planning

Brainstorming & Action Planning

Brainstorming & Action Planning

Brainstorming & Action Planning

Brainstorming & Action Planning

Brainstorming & Action Planning

Brainstorming & Action Planning

Brainstorming & Action Planning

Brainstorming & Action Planning

Brainstorming & Action Planning

Brainstorming & Action Planning

Brainstorming & Action Planning

Brainstorming & Action Planning

Brainstorming & Action Planning

Brainstorming & Action Planning

Write a brief summary about your action planning experience

Summary Continuation

CROSS-BRAND YOURSELF

For More Resources

Visit:

www.crossbrandingyounow.tumblr.com

www.amazon.com/author/alicianwaters

Or

To Book the Author

For Speaking Engagements

Email: www.anwempires@gmail.com

If you enjoyed this resource, please consider writing a review on Amazon.com

Thanks & Blessings!

CROSS-BRAND YOURSELF

www.ingramcontent.com/pod-product-compliance
Lightning Source LLC
Chambersburg PA
CBHW071823200526
45169CB00018B/926